W9-APV-609

THE SKELETON INSIDE YOU

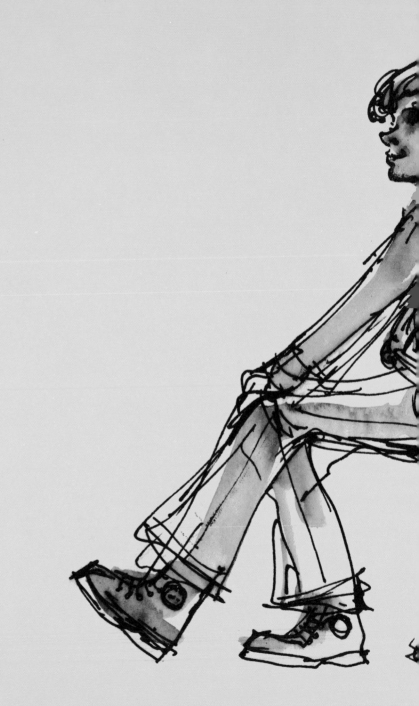

THE SKELETON INSIDE YOU

BY PHILIP BALESTRINO

Illustrated by Don Bolognese

A Harper Trophy Book
Harper & Row, Publishers

The *Let's-Read-and-Find-Out Book*™ series was originated by Dr. Franklyn M. Branley, Astronomer Emeritus and former Chairman of The American Museum–Hayden Planetarium, and was formerly coedited by him and Dr. Roma Gans, Professor Emeritus of Childhood Education, Teachers College, Columbia University. Text and illustrations for each of the more than 100 books in the series are checked for accuracy by an expert in the relevant field. The titles available in paperback are listed below. Look for them at your local bookstore or library.

Air Is All Around You
A Baby Starts to Grow
The BASIC Book
Bees and Beelines
Bits and Bytes
Comets
Corn Is Maize
Danger—Icebergs!
Digging Up Dinosaurs
Dinosaurs Are Different
A Drop of Blood
Ducks Don't Get Wet
Fireflies in the Night
Flash, Crash, Rumble, and Roll
Fossils Tell of Long Ago
Germs Make Me Sick!
Gravity Is a Mystery

Hear Your Heart
How a Seed Grows
How Many Teeth?
How to Talk to Your Computer
Hurricane Watch
Is There Life in Outer Space?
Look at Your Eyes
Me and My Family Tree
Meet the Computer
The Moon Seems to Change
My Five Senses
My Visit to the Dinosaurs
No Measles, No Mumps for Me
Oxygen Keeps You Alive
The Planets in Our Solar System
Rock Collecting
Rockets and Satellites

The Skeleton Inside You
The Sky Is Full of Stars
Snow Is Falling
Straight Hair, Curly Hair
Sunshine Makes the Seasons
A Tree Is a Plant
Turtle Talk
Volcanoes
Water for Dinosaurs and You
What Happens to a Hamburger
What I Like About Toads
What Makes Day and Night
What the Moon Is Like
Why Frogs Are Wet
Wild and Woolly Mammoths
Your Skin and Mine

The Skeleton Inside You
Text copyright © 1971 by Philip Balestrino
Illustrations copyright © 1971 by Don Bolognese
Printed in the U.S.A. All rights reserved.
Library of Congress Catalog Card Number: 85-42982
Trade ISBN 0-690-74122-7
Library ISBN 0-690-74123-5
Trophy ISBN 0-06-445039-2
Published in hardcover by Thomas Y. Crowell, New York.

THE SKELETON INSIDE YOU

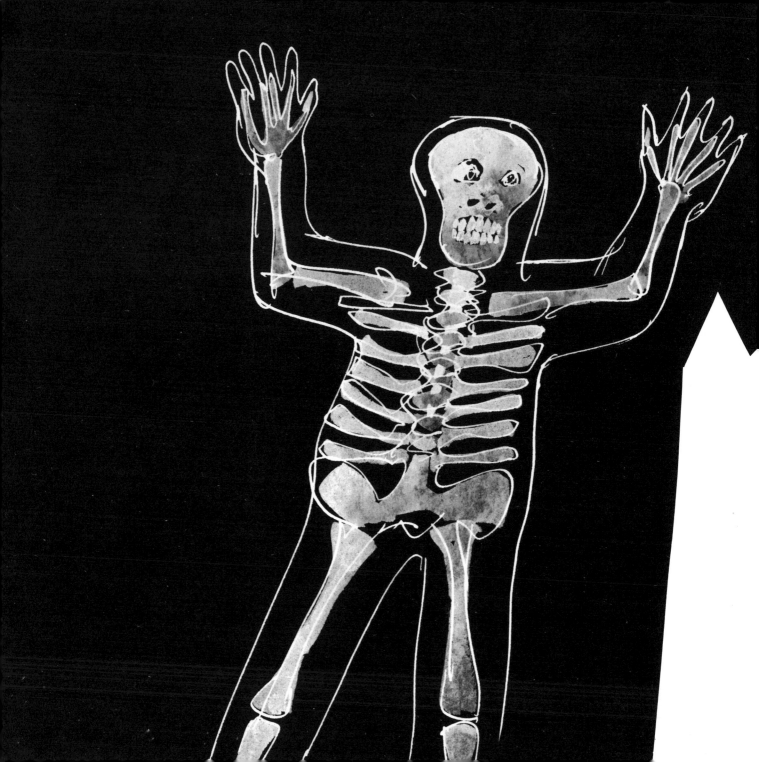

On Halloween I wore a skeleton costume. I used to think skeletons were made up just to scare people. Now I know that skeletons are real. They are not scary. I would not be me without a skeleton. You would not be you.

Skeletons are made up of many bones. Bones give you shape. A ball of clay has no bones inside it. You can make a ball of soft clay into any shape you want. You can make it into a little man. Then you can squash the man and roll him into a moustache or a snake. But nothing can change your shape, because you have a skeleton inside you.

A marionette has a skeleton, too, but it is made of wood and wire, not of real bones. A plain wooden chair is like a skeleton without any covering. When the chair is covered with stuffing and cloth, it is like your skeleton covered with muscles and skin. But your skeleton is different. It is made up of bones.

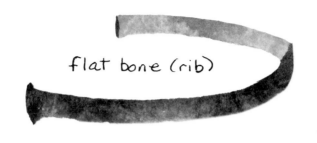

flat bone (rib)

small
bone
(finger)

Your skeleton is made up of 206 bones. There are
64 bones just in your two hands and arms. Some
of your bones are big, others are small. Some
bones are flat, others are round. Some of your
bones are soft, some are hard.

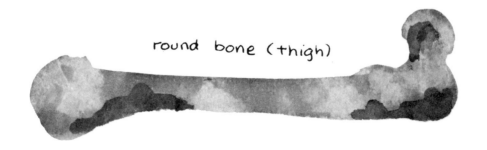

round bone (thigh)

Very soft bone is called cartilage. There is cartilage in your ears and nose. When the barber folds over your ear to cut your hair, your ear does not break off. That's because the soft cartilage in your ear can bend.

9

Once I pushed my nose flat against a bakery window to look at some cookies. My nose didn't hurt and it didn't break off. It came back to the same shape. Push your nose flat. It will bend, too, because it has soft bone inside it.

12

But most of your bones are hard. Sometimes they get broken. I fell out of a tree once and broke my arm. My mother took me to the doctor. The doctor took an X ray. Then he fitted the bone back together. Next the doctor put a stiff plaster cast on my arm to keep the bone together. I had a sling around my neck to hold my arm and the plaster cast. For several weeks I wore the cast. All the time, the bone was growing together. When the doctor took off the plaster cast my bone was all healed.

Bones live and grow just like every other part of the body. Bones start to grow before you are even born. As bones grow longer, you grow taller until you're all grown.

15

Foods like cheese and beef and milk have calcium in them. Calcium is a chemical that helps bones grow. Calcium also makes bones hard. Without it all your bones would be as soft as cartilage. They would be soft enough to tie into knots.

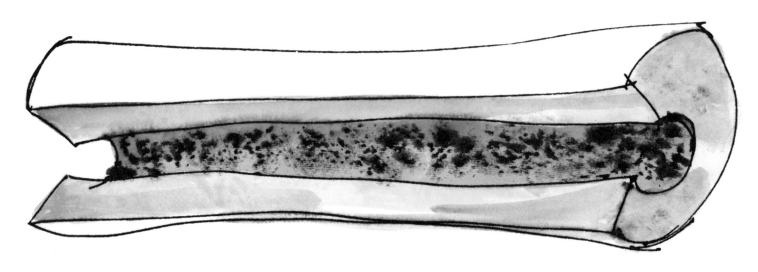

The centers of some hard bones are hollow. They
are filled with soft bone marrow. Bone marrow
helps make the red cells of your blood. Inside
some other bones is a spongy core. The core is

made up of hard bone and bone marrow. The insides of bones store many of the chemicals that come from the food you eat. These chemicals are saved up until your body needs them.

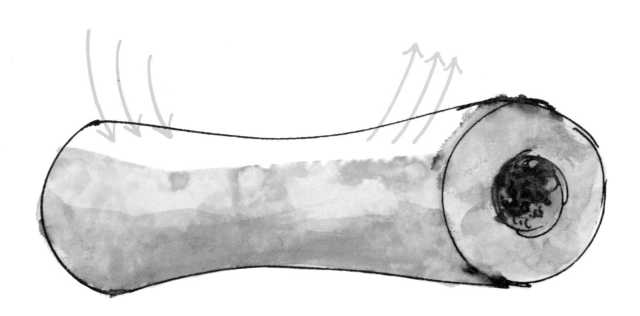

The butcher cut up a big soup bone for my mother.
The inside of it looked like this.

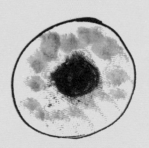

It was a bone from a big steer's leg. Your leg bones look almost the same inside.

All your 206 bones fit together to make your skeleton. Your skeleton helps you stand up straight. Without a skeleton, you would be like a ball of soft clay that can be molded into anything. You would be as floppy as a big beanbag.

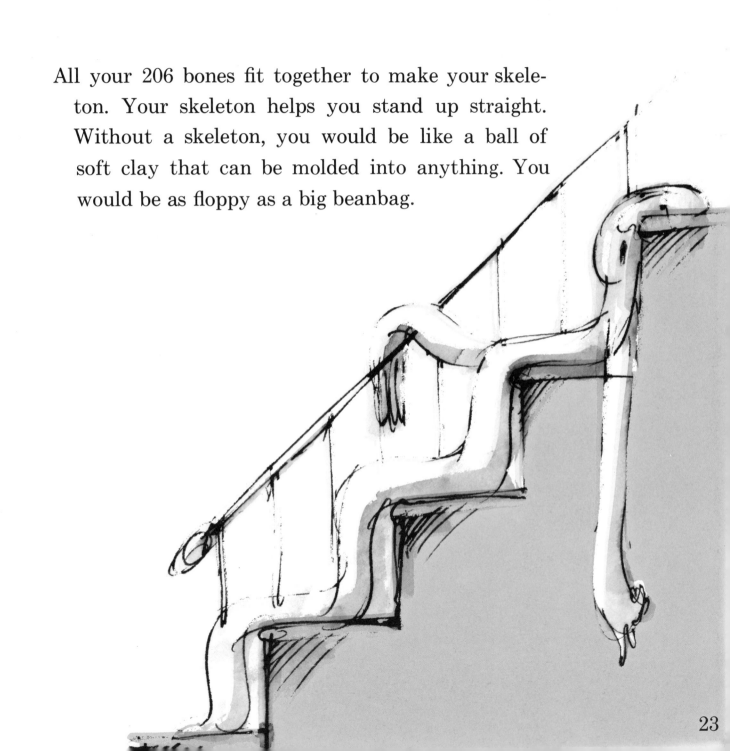

Some bones in your skeleton protect important parts inside you. Your rib bones cover your heart and lungs. Your skull protects your brain from hard knocks. The bones around your eyes protect them the way a football helmet does.

Your skeleton also helps you walk, run, and jump
and move in many ways.
The bones of your skeleton fit together at joints.

Without joints your skeleton could not move or bend. Elbows, ankles, and knees are joints. There are more than 200 joints in your skeleton. There are 56 joints in your hands alone.

The bones are held at the joints by ligaments. Ligaments are like strong, big rubber bands. They hold the bones at the joints, but they also stretch and let the bones move.

Your backbone is made up of 34 bones that fit together in 33 separate joints. That is why you can twist and turn almost any way. You can do a somersault. Or you can make yourself into a bridge, back up or belly up. If a backbone were only one bone, you could not do these things.

You could not put on a scary skeleton suit. You would not be able to run or jump or ring doorbells on Halloween if you did not have a skeleton inside you.

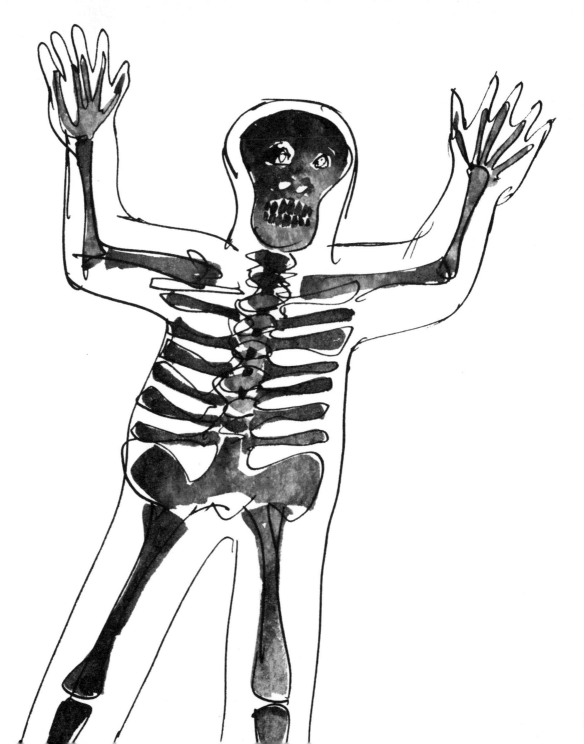

ABOUT THE AUTHOR

Philip Balestrino is a free-lance writer who lives in Manhattan with an English setter named Derf. Born in Brooklyn, Mr. Balestrino grew up on Long Island and went to college at Bucknell University in Pennsylvania, where he began writing plays for children and for adults. While working toward his master's degree in drama at The Catholic University of America in Washington, D.C., he helped establish a children's theater company for the city's poverty program.

In his leisure time, Mr. Balestrino enjoys exploring New York, collecting antique children's books, and playing long games of Monopoly.

ABOUT THE ARTIST

Don Bolognese was born in New York and was graduated from the Cooper Union School of Art, where he now teaches. Mr. Bolognese is the illustrator of many children's books, among them *Washington's Birthday*, a Crowell Holiday Book, and Clyde Robert Bulla's *The Ghost of Windy Hill*.

Don Bolognese and his family live in Brooklyn, New York, but summer in Vermont where they enjoy their hobby—hunting wild mushrooms.